Learning from the English Mystics

Alison Fry

Assistant Curate, St Peter with St Jude,
Milton, Weston-super-Mare

GROVE BOOKS LIMITED
RIDLEY HALL RD CAMBRIDGE CB3 9HU

Contents

Acknowledgement
I would like to record my grateful thanks to Dr Jan Rhodes
for her help in initiating my interest in this project.

The Cover Illustration is by Peter Ashton

First Impression February 1999
ISSN 0262-799X
ISBN 1 85174 395 2

1
Introduction

You have probably done it too. Something convinced you that you really ought to pray more. Spurred on by new-found enthusiasm you resolved to get up early and devote to God as much extra time as you could muster, so you set your alarm clock for an unfeasibly early (but very self-sacrificial) hour. By day three all your enthusiasm was in tatters and the sense of failure was complete as you crawled back to bed, promising to do better tomorrow, but of course tomorrow never came.

We think we *should* pray more. We think we *ought* to pray better but our best efforts seem destined to end in apparent failure. This is nothing new. More than 600 years ago an Englishman, Richard Rolle, wrote:

> 'You frequently awake early, so why don't you find him [that is, God] you say? Well surely, if you look for him in the right place, you are bound to find him.' *(The English Writings, The Commandment*, p 147)

We need some help to search in the right place.

Prayer is indeed a duty (1 Thessalonians 5.17, Luke 18.1) but it is also a delight and a joy (Psalm 37.4, Philippians 1.4) and neither (duty nor delight) can survive without the other. Our enthusiasm to get up early and pray more began with a longing for God and a wanting to delight in God. However, somehow that got lost in the 'shoulds' and 'oughts' of duty. If we are ever going to fulfil our longing for God we need to reach a point beyond the 'shoulds' and 'oughts' where we can 'want to want' to pray. We need some guidance to reach it.

Fortunately the resources already lie within our grasp.

> 'Our Lord has, in his great mercy, called you and led you to him by the desire of your heart…And so with his great grace he kindled your desire and fastened to it a leash of longing, and with this led you into a more special state and degree of life, to be a servant…of his.' *(The Cloud of Unknowing*, ch 1)

> 'There is delightful warmth in the loving heart…for there you, my God and my comfort, have set up your temple.' (Rolle, *Fire of Love*, ch 42)

Jesus promised, 'You did not choose me but I chose you' (John 15.16). Deep within our being God has built a temple (1 Corinthians 6.19), and from it God calls gently and urgently. The longing we feel, however fleeting, is our inner voice answering that call. The starting point to 'want to want' to pray is God's call, not our faltering response.

There is a God-shaped space in all our lives. But it is not one into which God can be plugged, like a piece in a jigsaw puzzle. Our God is too exciting to be pinned down and we grow and change as we are transformed by God. God is constantly revealing something new. So our yearning and longing and reaching out for God is renewed throughout our Christian journey. As we explore this journey our own resources are never enough. Sometimes we do not know which way to turn. Sometimes our longing loses its urgency. Then we need travelling companions, praying people who will join us for a part of the road which, though new for us, they know well.

The purpose of this booklet is to introduce one such group of companions—the so-called 'mediaeval English mystics.' They acted as helpers and guides to faithful people who were sincerely seeking God in their own day; they can help us still.

2

Who Were the English Mystics?

Many people have heard of John of the Cross and Teresa of Avila, the great 16th century continental mystics. They are acknowledged spiritual heavyweights. Yet it has never occurred to most people that there might be an English equivalent. Perhaps we are so used to English failure in the face of European competition (remember 'It's A Knockout'?) that it is easy to assume that the English score '*nil point*' on the scale of super-holiness.

Some will have heard of the 14th century Julian of Norwich, but may have no clear idea of who she was or why people get so excited about her writings. But few know that, contemporary with Julian, was a whole series of eminent English mystics. Highly regarded as spiritual teachers in their day, their writings have been prized for centuries after their deaths.

So let me introduce our travelling companions. Most of them never met each other in their own lifetimes and all have their own individual approach and style. All are at least 600 years old, so some of their habits, their ways of speaking or their assumptions may seem a little strange to us, as indeed our behaviour would astound them. But they share with us an earnest desire which is timeless—to love and to serve God and to share with others the riches of God's grace and gifts.

Richard Rolle (c1300–1349)

Rolle was probably born at Thornton in the Dale near Pickering. He was definitely not a dour Yorkshireman. He was an enthusiast, animated and passionate in the sheer excitement of his love for Jesus. Many would label him 'eccentric.'

Rolle seems always to have been a rebel. He left Oxford University before completing his Master's degree. At 19 he had returned to Yorkshire and run away from his parents to adopt the life of a hermit. This was perhaps his protest against a conventional church life, which did not seem to meet his very vivid experience of God. In his writings he is scathing about clerics whom he felt knew nothing of the love of God.

Hermits were sometimes members of a religious community but often they were individuals who lived in solitude in order to be more able to pray. Normally they were licensed by the diocesan bishop and supported themselves by performing a local service (often maintaining a stretch of road or a bridge). Rolle, of course, had to be unconventional. Apparently he had to borrow two of his sister's dresses to make a makeshift habit (such as hermits wore) because he was neither a member of a religious order nor licensed. The conventional rules of self-denial and asceticism did not appeal to Rolle. What mattered over and above all orthodoxy and legalities was a fervent devotion to God.

Without a Master's degree, he could not preach, teach or hold any major church or administrative office. Instead he relied on various patrons for support, and seems to have inspired deep affection among his friends and followers who included both high-ranking and unlearned lay folk. His anti-establishment, unconventional stance may explain his substantial popular appeal for a couple of centuries after his death—such attitudes were gaining ground as the Reformation approached.

His most famous work, *The Fire of Love*, was not addressed to anyone in particular but we know that Rolle acted as a spiritual guide to individuals (notably an anchoress, Margaret Kirkby, for whom his *Form of Living* was written) and to the Cistercian convent at Hampole near Doncaster, near to where Rolle ended his days.

The Bible was Rolle's primary authority—he peppered his work with scriptural quotations. He could be explosive in his opinions but also understanding and encouraging. He had an ability to joke at his own expense and is not insensitive. Rolle was a prolific writer in both Latin and English. Like the other English mystics, the English he wrote was that of his day—'middle English,' the language of Chaucer. This requires some translation to make it accessible today but modern versions are available of all the major works by the mystics.

Walter Hilton (died c1396)

Sadly we know very little about Hilton's life. We are not sure when or where he was born. He seems to have taken a degree at Cambridge and may have practised law for a time. His writings show him to have been a highly educated man with the precise, systematic and thoughtful mind of an academic theologian. His work also portrays someone of deep compassion and immense practical common sense.

Hilton probably became an Augustinian canon and spent his later life at the Priory at Thurgarton in Nottinghamshire. The Augustinians had a particular concern to bring God's word to 'the man in the street.' Hilton was no exception.

His major work, *The Scale of Perfection* (or *Ladder of Perfection*), was produced for a devout lay woman who had asked for guidance on living a life of contemplative prayer, and the *Mixed Life* was written for a layman seeking to make time for prayer in the midst of his responsibilities as the head of a mediaeval household. Hilton also makes it clear that he expected both works to be read more widely.

Hilton does not come across as the dry academic, scribbling from his ivory tower. He writes with care and pastoral concern for real people with real spiritual needs. His gentle and practical wisdom fits much more closely the role of a wise friend for the spiritual journey than an authoritative tutor schooling us in the way we should go.

The Cloud of Unknowing

We know still less about Hilton's contemporary, the author of *The Cloud of Unknowing* (c1370?). The generally accepted opinion is that he was probably a Carthusian monk and almost certainly a priest. Even today Carthusians are anonymous authors.

A number of works have been attributed to the same pen. These include *The Epistle of Privy Counsel* (or *A Letter of Private Direction*) and *The Epistle on Prayer*. Like Hilton he was a scholar whose advice and counsel had been sought by those for whom he wrote. He had the teacher's knack of explaining complex ideas with simplicity, a caustic sense of humour and a touch of the poet about him.

He writes with the conviction that God cannot be reached by human reason and is to that extent 'unknowable,' but God is accessible to love. Rational thought and careful study can only help us know *about* God. We only truly 'know' God when we love God and recognize that we are loved in return. The author of *The Cloud* gives the impression that he is struggling to communicate with inadequate human words and images what he has discovered of God in silence and stillness. His central certainty is that it is an absolute necessity to have God at the centre of one's life.

Julian of Norwich (c1342–c1416)

Julian lay close to death on 8–9 May 1373. She was gazing at a crucifix left by the priest, who had come to give her the last rites, when she received 16 'showings' or revelations from God. She recovered, and at some point in the next 30 years Julian wrote two accounts of these showings and her reflections on them. Her *Revelations of Divine Love* is the best known work of the English mystics and it is still much studied.[1] Because she is the least neglected of the English Mystics, Julian will remain in the background in this booklet to allow her contemporaries some limelight.

We do not know her real name. Julian was an anchoress associated with the church of St Julian and St Edward in Norwich and appears to have adopted the

---

1   See for example A Daffern, *The Cross and Julian of Norwich* (Grove Spirituality Series 46, 1993) and references in T Park, *The English Mystics: An Anthology* (London: SPCK, 1998).

saint's name. Anchorites were men and women who took vows to remain inside a cell for their natural life. They believed that cutting themselves off from the world enabled them to devote their lives to prayer. Many towns employed an anchorite specifically to pray for the town's welfare.

It may seem strange to us, but it was almost popular in the 14th century, particularly for devout, educated, urban, widows to adopt this lifestyle. Evidence suggests that it may have been less harsh and cramped than we might imagine. Anchoresses were warned to avoid extreme austerity in the 13th century work *The Ancrene Riwle*, or Rule for Anchoresses—a kind of handbook. They probably had a suite of rooms with a garden for growing provisions and need not live alone. Julian had at least two servants, Sara and Alice, and she would have been visited often by her parish priest and by pilgrims and others seeking her spiritual counsel. One such was Margery Kempe.

Margery Kempe (c1373–c1438)

Margery was a mediaeval housewife from King's Lynn, where her father was one-time mayor and Member of Parliament. Despite the status of her family Margery, like most lay people, was illiterate. A scribe wrote for her the autobiographical *Book of Margery Kempe*.

Many scholars have discarded Margery as a genuine English mystic because she does not quite fit the mould. This antipathy is partly the result of profound disappointment. Until 1934 only a few fragments of her work were known and these revealed her as another Mother Julian. The myth was exploded when a complete manuscript of the *Book of Margery Kempe* was unearthed in a private collection.

Margery was no holy anchoress, but a wife, mother to 14 children, an unsuccessful businesswoman and traveller. Her book begins with her own description of a bout of insanity after the birth of her first child. Today we would probably call it severe postnatal depression. Her spiritual life was marked by extreme emotion—incessant public tears, shouting, foretelling other people's damnation. She was tried for heresy twice and insisted on a vow of celibacy from her husband. The full book revealed someone who was 'an insensitive, completely self absorbed, bombastic and rather quarrelsome personality.'[2]

The revelations of the complete book led many to dismiss Margery as mad. The reputation has stuck, although it is not necessarily true. It was Margery's healing from madness that began her spiritual explorations. She was driven to tears by penitence for her own sins and those of the world, and by an acute awareness of Christ's passion and suffering—which ought to be something to shout about!

Although her behaviour startles us, it was accepted by the church authorities in her day. Heresy charges against her were never upheld. The worst accusation she sustained from her contemporaries was that she was putting it on. Margery

2   S Bhattacharji, *God is an Earthquake* (London: DLT, 1997) p xviii.

was a devout and articulate laywoman, with energy and ambition, but illiterate and barred from the religious life by marriage. How else might she have expressed her overwhelming desire to serve God with heart, mind, soul and strength?

Of all the English mystics, Margery remained the one most in touch with everyday life. She tried to live faithfully in the world, not shut away from it. Rather than being a spiritual consultant, she consulted—anchorites, hermits and other prayerful people. It is perhaps the very 'ordinariness' of her life that is appealing.

The unprecedented wealth of spiritual writing that this odd assorted group has left may relate to the world they lived in. It was a time of great upheaval. The 100 years war (1337–1453) drained the country. The great plague of 1348–49 killed a third of the population. The discontent which exploded in the Peasant's Revolt of 1381, sparked by poll taxes, was brewing. The seeds of the great changes of the Reformation were in the wind. Parliament was disputing the payment of papal taxes. John Wycliffe and the Lollards were questioning the nature of the eucharist, the authority of the clergy and the use of Scriptures solely in Latin. Executions by burning for religious opinions were common.

The English mystics seem to have responded to the spiritual needs that people were feeling in this uncertain climate. Our world may be very different from theirs but we too live in a confusing time of loss, conflict, change and spiritual need. The English mystics offer some wisdom which spans the centuries.

3

A Word About Mysticism

A reputation, whether good or bad, is very hard to shift and the word 'mystic' has a reputation. It conjures up a picture in many people's minds of a turban-clad guru. 'Mysticism' has attached to it various esoteric and mysterious practices ranging from horoscopes and fortune telling to Stonehenge and the druids. Mysticism is often associated with eastern religions or groups on the fringes of the mainstream. It seems to belong to strange and alien cultures. This is a reputation that is difficult to change, even though we know that it is a caricature.

Yet there is a long history of *Christian* mysticism. It extends from the pages of Scripture into the lives of all who seek to know and serve their Lord. Christian mysticism is not about chanting mantras, but singing hymns and psalms and spiritual songs. It is not about physical and breathing exercises, but about discipline in prayer. It is not about focussing on a single object until it occupies the whole of one's consciousness; it is about being preoccupied with God. It is not seeking an experience of heightened awareness, but an exploration of fellowship with Father, Son and Holy Spirit.

For the English mystics the word 'mysticism' would have had none of today's connotations. All the accumulated baggage of the intervening centuries needs to be jettisoned. Only then can we hear what the English mystics actually said about mysticism instead of what we fear they may have said.

Mystic and mysticism are derived from the Greek *mystikos*, a word referring to things which are hidden. For the English mystics, 'mysticism' referred to meeting Christ hidden in the Scriptures and the sacraments but revealed through the work of the Holy Spirit.[3] In any case they tended to refer to their way of life as 'contemplative' not 'mystical.' Christian mysticism might simply be described as the journey towards a place of contemplative prayer.

Perhaps, therefore, we would be more comfortable with the word 'contemplation' instead of 'mysticism' and to speak of 'a contemplative' instead of 'a mystic.' The two words are used interchangeably when speaking of Christian mysticism. Their meaning may be the same but the reputation of the words is different. With 'contemplation' we are in the realms of peace and tranquillity, of walking with our God beside still waters, in the silence of eternity.

Many of us have been there, albeit briefly. Deep in prayer we suddenly catch a glimpse of the nearness of God; in the middle of a moving church service we sense vividly his presence and peace. This is a glimmer of what the English mystics would have called 'contemplation.'

It sounds idyllic but it is not a place that is easy to find, especially in a frantic, restless, rush-filled world. The experience comes to us out of the blue and we do not know how to find our way there again. There never seems to be enough time to stop and pray when there's work to be done, the children need collecting from school and the supper is still in the supermarket!

So is 'the contemplative' something to leave to the experts? It is true that those who have, down the ages, been called 'mystics' or 'contemplatives' were regarded as people with a special gift from God for contemplation. They can seem to be on a higher plain that the rest of us because of a special calling or vocation from God to a contemplative lifestyle. Yet these 'experts' have spent an extraordinary amount of energy trying to help other 'ordinary' people follow the same path.

The English mystics wrote books by hand, at a time before the printing press was invented, when paper (or parchment) was scarce and expensive. They wrote in English when writing spiritual works in the vernacular ran the risk of imprisonment or burning. Their enthusiasm in their efforts to encourage their fellow-Christians to journey towards a deeply reflective relationship with God is evident from their work. They believed that at least a degree of contemplative prayer is available to all and they did not seem to regard themselves as distinguished contemplatives.

---

3   T Park, *op cit*, p 6.

4
What is Contemplative Prayer?

In mediaeval understanding, the contemplative life was distinguished from the active life. There were

'...two manner of states...in Holy Church, by which Christian souls please God and get them the bliss of heaven: the one is bodily and the other is ghostly.'

(Hilton, *Mixed Life*, ch 1)

This does not mean that salvation was sought through works. Hilton writes here of *Christian* souls who he assumed were already saved. Rather there were two equally valid paths towards sanctification. The *Ancrene Riwle* puts it less controversially:

'...the rules of this pursuit are two. The first is concerned with the right directing of the heart, the second with the right ordering of exterior things.' (p 1)

The *active life* was one path, which

'...lies in love and charity shown outwardly in good bodily works, in the fulfilment of God's commandments and of the seven works of mercy—bodily and spiritual—towards one's fellow Christians.'

(Hilton, *Scale of Perfection*, bk 1, ch 2)

The seven bodily works of mercy were: feed the hungry, give drink to the thirsty, clothe the naked, visit the prisoner, shelter the stranger, visit the sick and to bury the dead (Matthew 25.31ff). The spiritual mercies were to correct the sinner, teach the ignorant, counsel the doubtful, comfort the sorrowful, bear wrongs patiently, forgive all injuries and to pray for the living and departed, all of which have scriptural precedent. The active life also included activities such as holding vigils and fasting.

So the active life involved ordering one's outward, bodily affairs, in accordance with God's word and might easily have been summarized as 'loving your neighbour.'

The *contemplative life* was the other path. By contrast to the active life, this concerned the ordering of one's inner, or spiritual, affairs.

The ultimate gift of the contemplative life was the state of mystical union with God. This could only truly be obtained the other side of the grave but it could be approached in this life. The author of *The Cloud of Unknowing* explains:

'My spiritual friend in God, you are to understand that according to our rather crude reckoning, there are four degrees and forms of the Christian life...Three of these can be begun and ended in this life, and one may begin the fourth by grace here below, which is to last without end in the happiness of heaven.'

(ch 1)

Hilton also helps get our 20th-century minds round this. He explains that the contemplative life has several parts which approximate to the 'degrees' the author of *The Cloud* mentions above.

a) 'The first lies in the knowledge of God and the things of the spirit acquired by reason, by the teaching of man and by the study of holy Scripture.'

(*Scale*, bk 1, ch 4)

Some have a particular calling to be scholars who are devoted 'long study and labour in holy Scripture,' but it is in measure open to all Christian people, 'to good and bad alike.'

b) Hilton knows that knowledge without love is worthless (1 Corinthians 13.2), so

'The second part of contemplation lies principally in affection'

(*Scale*, bk 1, ch 5)

that is, the will to give oneself to serve God, or simply devotion.

'Sometimes a man or woman meditating on God feels a fervour of love and spiritual sweetness in the remembrance of his passion, or any of his works in his humanity; or he feels great trust in the goodness and mercy of God for the forgiveness of sins, and for his gifts of grace…He cannot explain what it is, but he feels it plainly…making him feel that he does not care what then becomes of him provided the will of God is fulfilled.' (*Scale*, bk 1, ch 5)

Devotion is open to all Christian people in the 'active life' in, as Hilton terms it, a 'lower degree.' A 'higher degree' 'can be had and held only by people who are in great quietness of body and soul' (*Scale*, bk 1, ch 7). By this he appears to mean that, although all may find it, it can only be 'held' (sustained) by those who have chosen to devote themselves to the contemplative life—such as those in religious orders, anchorites and hermits. Practice makes perfect it seems.

c) The final part of contemplation

'…which is as perfect as can be here, lies both in cognition and in affection; that is to say, in the knowing and perfect loving of God. That is when a person's soul is first cleansed from all sins and reformed to the image of Jesus by completeness of virtues, and afterward he is visited and taken up from all earthly and fleshly affections, from vain thoughts and imaginations of all bodily things, and is as if forcibly ravished out of the bodily sense; and then is illumined by the grace of the Holy Spirit to see intellectually the Truth, which is God, and also spiritual things, with a soft, sweet burning love for him.'

(*Scale*, bk 1, ch 8)

This perfect knowing and loving of God is again available to all, whether in an active or contemplative life, but only by God's special gift and grace. The mystics could teach contemplation but only God could give the 'mystical' experience of union with himself. This is vital to the Christian understanding of mysticism.

Both Hilton and the author of *The Cloud* issue spiritual health warnings. No one is to seek after such experiences. They specifically dismiss any seeking after physical sensations in which they seem to be having a dig at the excesses of their predecessor, Richard Rolle. He describes the fire of his love for God as warming his heart:

'It was real warmth too, not imaginary, and it felt as if it were actually on fire. I was astonished at the way the heat surged up and how this new and unexpected sensation brought great and unexpected comfort.'

(Fire, Prologue, p 45)

and appears to think that physical sensations demonstrate the highest devotion:

'It would be surprising if anyone without such experience should claim the name of contemplative.'   *(Fire, ch 2)*

God will speak to our individual and unique personalities but we should be wary of seeking any particular physical or spiritual sensation. It is God we are seeking, not an experience.

The Mixed Life

Because the English mystics aimed to help their readers towards the contemplative path, it can appear that they thought this path was a more important, higher and better way. We seem to have gone to the opposite extreme. It is active life that counts, not just in our world but in our churches too. If I announced to my congregation that I was called to a contemplative life, while remaining in my post as curate, I suspect they would feel that they were being short-changed and that I was malingering. After all, there is the Sunday school to oversee, the visiting to be done, the services to prepare…all kinds of activity.

Jesus at Bethany told Martha 'Mary has chosen the good portion' (Luke 10.42). This need not be translated as 'better portion' as some would have it, but the implication is that Jesus wants his followers to have the opportunity to set aside their busy-ness and sit and listen to him.

In reality the active and contemplative paths cannot be entirely separated. The English mystics recognized this. Just as the contemplative life required the ordering of one's outward and active life, the contemplative life could also be brought into the active. Hilton had a specific pastoral concern for one lay person with many responsibilities who was not free to devote his entire life to contemplation but nonetheless

'…yearnest greatly to serve our Lord by ghostly occupation all wholly, without letting or troubling of worldly business, that thou mightest come by grace to more knowing and ghostly [spiritual] feeling of God and of ghostly things.'

(Mixed Life, ch 2)

Hilton was certain that the active life was as much a path to God as the contemplative life. Loving God was not the prerogative of the professional contemplative. The journey to self understanding and awareness of the gift of salvation in Christ, as well as the journey to active love for one's neighbour, were both central to all Christian devotion.

People whose lives are professionally devoted to God—the vicar, the nun, or the missionary—can seem to be capable of a deeper faith or greater heights of prayer than other Christians. We still need to recognize that such 'professional' Christians are merely called to express their devotion in a *particular* way, not in a *higher* or *better* way that is inaccessible to others. This misconception does not escape the caustic humour of the author of the *Epistle of Privy Counsel*:

> 'Through their blindness and sophistication people have no more insight and understanding of these simple exercises [contemplative prayer] than the child at his ABC has of the knowledge of the greatest scholar in the university...Yet in truth it is this simple exercise that can unite the soul of the most uncouth man alive to God in love and humility and perfect charity.' (ch 1)

Contemplative prayer is there for absolutely anyone!

More importantly Hilton recognized that a desire for the contemplative life was in the gift of God. God sometimes gave it to those who were not 'professional' contemplatives but who had worldly responsibilities. In these circumstances it was not necessary to rush to the nearest monastery or hermitage. When we feel drawn to spend time in quiet, contemplative prayer in the midst of our busy lives we are to live what Hilton calls the 'mixed life,' that is,

> '...sometimes to use the works of mercy in active life, in help and sustenance of themselves, and of their subjects, and of others also; and sometimes for to leave all manner of outward business, and give themselves unto prayers and meditations, reading of Holy Writ, and to other ghostly occupations...'
>
> (*Mixed Life*, ch 5)

If we were to forsake our worldly business we would fail in our responsibility to love our neighbour. Equally, to forsake contemplation would be to deny a God-given gift.

The mixed life may seem to be the perfect example of an English compromise, but there is good biblical precedent for spending some time in one practice and some in another (Ecclesiastes 3.1–9). More than one mystic suggests becoming like *both* Martha and Mary. And of course Jesus himself chose to spend some time on earth and, while here, to devote some time to prayer and solitude (for example, Mark 1.35), and some in active work.

Most Christians today have a limited amount of time to devote to prayer and meditation on Scripture. Most of us are not members of religious orders or ordained (and so in a sense paid to pray). But neither are we uninterested in prayer and contemplation. We need to find the right balance between our outer, active life and our inner, contemplative life. This search is what fired the English mystics.

5
'Go Then Alone…'

The English mystics have gained the title 'mystics' because of their writing on contemplative prayer, and their own evident experience of God's grace and blessing received through it. However, this was not their only consideration. Much of what we can learn from them concerns the basic discipline of prayer. None of the English mystics consider contemplative prayer in isolation. It is, for them, only a part of a whole pattern of prayer.

The first problem is to carve out a time and place. No prayer, whether intercessory or contemplative, individual or corporate, can happen without making space for it and the English mystics knew that only in solitude is it possible to devote all our energies to contemplative prayer. They urge their readers to 'go then alone to thy prayers and to thy meditations' (*Mixed Life*, ch 11), or

> 'Whoever has this gift of God fervently needs to escape for the time from the presence and company of everyone, and to be alone, lest he should be hindered.'
> (*Scale*, bk 1, ch 30)

> 'Their sole desire is for the joys which are eternal and so they make time for devotion and contemplation, never wavering in their wholehearted effort to love Christ. Many of their number, although they live physically among people, are mentally remote from them.'
> (*Fire*, ch 13)

Finding a place of solitude for prayer has biblical roots. Jesus took time alone to pray before many of his most important choices (Matthew 4.1ff; 14.13, 23; 26.36ff and parallels; Luke 6.12). He taught his followers to withdraw from the business of life and pray alone (Matthew 6.6; Mark 6.31). If God is moving us to spend time with him, we must not let ourselves be drawn away by distractions. When a friend asks us to join them for an evening, we try to keep our promise even if a better offer comes along. Times of solitude and silence guard our relationship with God.

We need a place where we shall be undisturbed but the time need not be long—ten minutes on the walk to work, in the traffic queue, or during a coffee break. There are many pauses that go unnoticed during our busy days that we could claim as time for God. Several of the mystics recommend either first thing in the morning or closing the day with a review of its activities. Generations of Christians have found this helpful. The important thing is to make sure that the space is feasible and sustainable. It is pointless to set unattainable targets. My piano teacher used to insist that five minutes practice daily was better than half an hour once a week. I suspect that the same is true for 'practising the presence of God,' though it is also appropriate to find longer now and again, perhaps on a holiday or a retreat.

Avoiding the distractions of the world is only half of the benefit of solitude. In a curious way, avoiding temptations brings us face to face with our own short-comings. Once we have set aside the preoccupations that fill our lives, we are left alone to confront God and have God confront us. Solitude forces us to face our own state before God, and so allows God to deal with us.

Solitude may seem a very uncomfortable prospect. This is partly because it is so unfamiliar and we are all a little bit afraid of the unknown. We have driven out almost all space for solitude and silence in our busy, noisy world. At home the television or the radio are turned on, shops and work places are filled with 'muzak,' the headphones of a 'Walkman' are carefully positioned to shut out silence.

Solitude also appears uncomfortable because we are afraid of loneliness and isolation, of being alone. But that is not at all the same thing as solitude. Rolle writes:

'They define "alone" not as being "without God," but understand it to mean "without company." A man is alone indeed if God is not with him.' (*Fire*, ch 13) If we never face our inmost being or God, we will never allow ourselves to be truly as we are, however 'foul and wretched' (*Epistle of Privy Counsel*, ch 2) we may be; nor can we allow God to be as God is. We are then less than the human beings we were created to be. We are not in union with our creator. We are still running away from the guilt of the garden of Eden. Part of the goal of contempla-tive prayer is to be open and honest within the security of our relationship with Christ. The mystics suggest that solitude is a place to

'...take good, gracious God just as he is, and without further ado lay him on your sick self just as you are, for all the world as if he were a poultice! Or to put it in other words, lift up your sick self just as you are, and through your long-ing strive to touch good, gracious God just as he is. Touching him is eternal health, which is the point of the story of the woman in the Gospel who said,..."If I touch but the hem of his garment I shall be whole."'

(*Epistle of Privy Counsel*, ch 2)

Once we have found this peace, silence and solitude can be carried into the noisi-est of circumstances. Hilton hints at this in urging his reader, if he is interrupted by the call of his family or work to

'...leave off lightly thy devotion, whether it be in prayer or in meditation, and go do thy debt and thy service to thine even-Christians [fellow Christians] as readily as if our Lord himself bade thee do so...' (*Mixed Life*, ch 10)

Solitude will not rob us of precious time which we could spend doing all sorts of useful activities. Rather, peace and stillness will fill our lives—and may draw others towards our God who grants us such serenity, as Margery Kempe found:

'Many...wanted to hear her converse, for her conversation was so much to do with the love of God that those who heard it were often moved to weep very sadly.' (*Book of Margery Kempe*, bk 1, ch 16)

15

6

'…Unto Prayers and Meditations'

One reason for our reluctance to seek solitude and silence may be that we are not sure what to do with it once we have got it. We are uncertain how to go about silent or contemplative prayer.

It is easy to equate prayer with intercession. Even biblical translators make this mistake. The word usually translated 'intercession' or 'petition' in Hebrews 7.25 ('since he always lives to make intercession for them' and also in Romans 8.27, 34 and 11.2) actually primarily means 'to fall in with,' 'to meet with in order to converse,' 'to turn to'—phrases which encompass a relationship between two persons involving listening and responding to one another. It is this biblical aspect of prayer that the English mystics can help us reclaim. They guide us towards the unfamiliarity of contemplative prayer through more familiar patterns of prayer.

Confession was fundamental to all prayer for the English mystics. Turning to face God inevitably makes us aware of our shortcomings.

> 'God's word, whether written or spoken, is like a mirror…It follows, then, that when a person sees in the bodily or spiritual mirror, or knows by the information he gets from someone else, just where the dirty mark is on his bodily or spiritual face, he goes to the well to wash it off—and not before. Now if this mark is a particular sin, the well is holy Church and the water confession, with all its elements. And if the mark is simply the blind root with the impulse to sin, then the well is the merciful God, and the water is prayer, with all its elements.' (*Cloud*, ch 35)

Confession was assumed to include a formal confession before a priest because this was the practice of the day and of the religious communities to which several of the mystics belonged. However, Hilton explicitly states that confession can be a private act of contrition before God (*Mixed Life*, ch 17), Margery Kempe describes doing so (*Book of Margery Kempe*, ch 5), and Rolle provides an example, and is soon soaring heavenwards:

> 'When a man, devout and poor, worries over his sin, he can pray (if he so desires) like this: Jesus Christ, my Lord and God, take pity on me; please consider my body's grievous yoke, which depresses my soul so quickly. My flesh is faltering under the burdens of life, and in consequence my spiritual strength is flagging too. For all that the world ever gave me I have spent, and now nothing remains but for you to lead my soul to that other world where my most precious treasure, where my real and lasting wealth abides…For truly my treasure is you, yourself.' (*Fire*, ch 16)

The First Degree of Prayer was what followed confession for Hilton:
> 'You are to understand that there are three kinds of prayer. The first is spoken
> prayer.' *(Scale*, bk 1, ch 26–27)

He took it for granted that the vocal, daily, recited, formal prayers of the church
were a part of his reader's life. Admittedly most of the mystics were themselves
members of religious orders where set prayers were an obligation. *The Ancrene
Riwle* devotes so much space to this that it is difficult to see how the anchoresses
had time to eat never mind make lace—one of their edifying pastimes! We cannot
match such diligence but it is possible to focus on saying
> '...thy *Pater Noster*, or thine *Ave*, or else thy *Matins*, or else for to read upon thy
> Psalter. For that is evermore a secure standard that will not fail: Whoso may
> cleave thereto, he shall not err.' *(Mixed Life*, ch 29)

Such prayers were 'the first degree' because they were the foundation for all other
forms of prayer. The mystics believed that formal, spoken prayers were the best
forms of prayer for a person beginning a spiritual life, acting as 'a firm staff to
support him.'

We have to start somewhere. Prayers gleaned from Scripture, or honed by
centuries of faithful people at worship, give us a language with which to begin.
We learn to speak, read and write initially by imitation. Only later do we find our
own words. The same is true of learning to pray and of exploring new ways of
praying. We borrow other people's prayers to equip us with the tools that then
enable us to discover our own voice in prayer.

Furthermore someone else's written prayers can often express things we cannot ourselves find the words for. Such prayers guard against the danger that
> '...in the quiet of their meditation they imagine and think of spiritual things
> according to their own wit...Therefore through their indiscretion they often
> overstrain their wits and break the powers of their body, and so fall into fanta-
> sies and singular inventions, or into manifest errors...If they only knew how
> little they feel in comparison with what God gives...they would be ashamed...'
> *(Scale*, bk 1, ch 28)

The habit of formal, spoken prayers can be a life-belt at times when prayer is
hard, or we do not want to pray:
> '...should your prized facility of prayer or meditation desert you and you
> cannot raise your mind to joyful and holy contemplation or sing as you once
> did, you are not on that account to give up your reading or praying or what-
> ever other useful thing you do, be it outward or inward, lest you degenerate
> into sloth.' *(Fire*, ch 10)

The English mystics also help us reclaim our memory here. We tend to read our
formal prayers out of books and to assume that most other people can too. The
mystics lived in an era before the printing press was invented. There were few
books and fewer to read them. They assumed that set prayers would be recited
from memory. Searching within oneself for the words must have made the prayers
more vital than chanting them out of a book.

In spite of increased literacy, the majority in our society belongs to what has been dubbed the 'non-book culture.' A minority actually buys books and reads them. Our churches have a responsibility to teach people a few memorable prayers that can be learned by heart and carried anywhere (such as the Lord's Prayer). If we do not, the whole language of prayer from which could spring the individual's own prayer and spiritual life will literally be a closed book. We will risk depriving people of all spiritual resources.[4]

The Second Degree of Prayer went a step further. Formal, spoken prayers need not be boring. Set prayers allow us to search the heights and depths of written prayers, whether scriptural, liturgical, or other people's wisdom. They are a fuel which sustains our fire of devotion:

> '...nourish the fire of love in [your] heart with holy psalms, pure thoughts, fervent desires, so that it never goes out.'   (*Scale*, ch 32)

They are a springboard to 'the second degree of prayer.' For Hilton this

> '...is spoken, but without any particular set words, and this is when a man or a woman feels the grace of devotion by the gift of God, and in his devotion speaks to him as if he were bodily in his presence.'   (*Scale*, bk 1, ch 29)

Christians today often value such extempore prayer as a 'first degree.' There is nothing wrong in that. The empty recitation of meaningless words is frowned upon in the Scriptures (Matthew 6.5–8). Whether in our own words or someone else's, what is vital is our attitude when we pray:

> '...don't be concerned about how much you are reciting, but rather how well, so that the love of your heart may always be directed upward, and your thought on what you are saying, as far as you are able.' (Rolle, *A Form of Living*, ch 7)

Extempore prayer is triggered and enriched by formal, written or remembered prayer.

The Third Degree of Prayer is wordless adoration:

> '...I was sitting in that same chapel, and repeating as best I could the night-psalms before I went to supper...In my prayer I was reaching out to heaven with heartfelt longing when I became aware, in a way I cannot explain, of a symphony of song, and in myself I sensed a corresponding harmony at once wholly delectable and heavenly, which persisted in my mind.'   (*Fire*, ch 15)

It is difficult for us with our 20th century, activist lifestyles to see the point of this kind of silent adoration. Surely reciting the Lord's Prayer or the psalms and adding our own intercessions or words of praise is enough! Should not we be out there, active, doing something? Yet across the centuries we read:

> 'Your wayward curiosity can find nothing solid to hold on to in a happening of this sort, and so it grumbles and tells you to stop doing it and do something "useful" in the curious way people understand it—for it seems to these that

---

4   See G Pigott, *Prayers to Remember* (Grove Spirituality Series 52, 1995).

what you are doing is not at all important: they do not know the first thing about it!'   (*Epistle of Privy Counsel*, ch 2)

'And though all your bodily faculties can find there nothing to feed on because they think that what you are doing is nothing, carry on, then, with that nothing, as long as you are doing it for God's love. Do not leave off, but press on earnestly in that nothing with an alert desire in your will to have God...'
                                                                                    (*Cloud*, ch 68)
Why? Because
'Prayer in itself is nothing but a devout reaching out directly to God, in order to attain the good and to do away with evil.'   (*Cloud*, ch 39)
We are summoned to love God with, mind and heart, strength and soul. Sometimes this will take the form of Bible study, sometimes singing his praises, sometimes loving our neighbour, but sometimes love goes beyond words. The English mystics often use the image of the Christian soul united to her bridegroom, Christ. Just as in a human relationship words are not always the best way to express our love so with this 'marriage' for which we were created. Margery Kempe found that all the wise words in Rolle and Hilton did not express her experience of God (*Book of Margery Kempe*, bk1, ch 17). The living God exceeds description, and our relationship with God will not always need words.

Wordless adoration is perhaps the closest we come to 'praying continually' (1 Thessalonians 5.17; Hebrews 13.15). Obviously it is not possible to focus our thoughts upon God every waking second:

'I do not say that you should persevere in it [contemplation] with the same vigour; for that is not possible. Sometimes sickness or other disorders of body or soul, and many other necessities of nature, will greatly hinder you...But I do say that you should always be either doing it or preparing for it; that is to say either actually or in intention.'   (*Cloud*, ch 41)

Rather the mystics understood 'pray continually' to mean that, through regular and deliberate contemplative devotion we would develop a habit of desiring God. Contemplative prayer enables us to adopt an attitude that is pointing continually in God's direction.

7
'Reading of Holy Writ'

Contemplative prayer is not divorced from our whole pattern of prayer. Neither is it the emptying of one's mind. The English mystics do not expect our contemplation to start with a blank sheet. Reading and studying Scripture is part of the pattern of prayer.

Cyprian, the 3rd century bishop of Carthage, wrote: 'in prayer you speak to God, in reading God speaks to you.' Such scriptural conversation was the source of the continual awareness of God for which the mystics aimed. Something carefully read and prayed will pop up throughout the day. The author of *The Cloud* wrote:

'...there are certain preparatory exercises which should occupy the attention of the contemplative apprentice: the lesson, the meditation and the petition. They may be called, for better understanding, reading, reflecting and praying.'
(*Cloud*, ch 35)

This will be familiar to some as the 'Lectio Divina,'[5] that is, reading, meditation and prayer, leading towards contemplation. It is no ordinary 'reading.' First the subject matter is prescribed—the Scriptures, and possibly other devotional works. Then, the manner of reading. It is to be slow and attentive. Not searching for information from the passage but listening for God's voice speaking from it.

Such meditation is more than merely reflecting quietly and prayerfully on the passage. It may include reading several times, allowing words and phrases to speak to us. It may mean imaginatively entering a biblical scene (Margery Kempe frequently reports her somewhat fanciful imaginings). Or a verse or phrase is consciously repeated—carried about throughout the day. Prayer (petition, thanksgiving, praise) grows from such reflections as a response to what we have 'heard' in the text.

Faced with the whole Bible it can be difficult to decide where to begin. Hilton suggested a series of subjects for meditation—the Passion of Jesus or his life on earth and his humanity (*Mixed Life*, ch 19–27). The lives of saints, especially the saints of the Scriptures (Peter, Paul, and various Marys) could also be an inspiration. They were to aid contemplation only in so far as they help to focus on the divinity of Christ, and thence direct our thoughts to God.

We might equally choose a passage from our daily Bible reading notes or something in our mind from a Sunday sermon. God will already be at work in our choice:

'...the spiritual presence of Jesus opens the understanding of his lover who burns in desire for him, and by the ministry of angels brings to his mind the

---

5 For a fuller treatment see T Hall, *Too Deep for Words* (New York: Paulist Press, 1991) pp 36ff.

words and the insights of holy Scripture, unsought and unconsidered, one after another, and readily expounds them, however hard or secret they may be.'
(Scale, bk 2, ch 43)

These 'preparatory exercises' do not automatically lead to contemplation in the technical sense. They are our human activities directed towards God. True contemplation is only in God's gift. It can never be attained by sheer effort or obedience to patterns and techniques or silence, reading and meditation.

'By God's grace you will transform a duty into a delight.' (*Mixed Life*, ch 27)

Each of us is a unique individual and our creator will deal with us each in our own way. Prayer is not to be a straitjacket:

'...not that thou shalt use the same form alway that I say, but that thou should have thereby...some warning and wissing [instruction, direction] for to rule thee in thy occupation...Which are best for thee can I not say.'
(Mixed Life, ch 16–17)

The mystics' instructions are to form a framework from which the individual can explore his or her own relationship with God.

8
Mysticism Revisited

We have discovered the English mystics to be deeply committed Christian people. They received God's grace and gifts and attempted to share these with their neighbour. They still show, through their writings, the desire for their fellow Christians to join them on their contemplative journey. Their insight can be as fresh and vital today as it was over 600 years ago.

The English mystics have taught us that prayer is not primarily intercession. It is meeting with God on our journey through and towards his kingdom and learning to align ourselves in prayer with God's wants and wishes for his world. Archbishop Michael Ramsey, who was much influenced by the English mystics, wrote that contemplative prayer

'...was not only a quest for the inner peace of God but an exposure to the love of God with intercessory outreach.'[6]

The mystics have shown us that contemplative prayer does not divorce the Christian from the world, and it is not performed in a vacuum. Contemplation has a place only within a context of prayer, Bible study, love of God and our neighbour. It is a context which we cannot achieve in total seclusion. Times of solitude and silence are but a part of our wider involvement in the worshipping community—the church.

Some are called to devote themselves to contemplative prayer and join appropriate religious communities. Most of us are called to pray as we can, not as we cannot—to direct our lives towards God in contemplation as far as we are able. There will be times of difficulty and darkness as we seek to probe the mystery that is God. But the person of Jesus Christ is our focus and the glorious dawn of his resurrected presence is our encouragement in our endeavours.

Contemplation may grow into a vivid experience of God's nearness, an intense awareness of God and our relationship with him. It is a God-given insight which, if anything, is what might be termed the 'mystical experience.' However,

'...the effect of the experience...is not to cause a person to long to have the experience again but to serve God and to do his will. Those who have had mystic experience will not want to tell everyone about it; they will have a longing to serve God in daily life, for his *will* is our peace.'[7]

Hilton warned his reader not to attempt to grasp the moment of meditative union so much that other duties suffered (*Mixed Life*, chs 30–31), nor are we to be kept from sleep, food or other duty by our meditation—prayer is not to become an

---

6   M Ramsey, *Be Still and Know* (London: Fount Paperbacks, 1982) p 13.
7   M Ramsey, *Canterbury Pilgrim* (London: SPCK, 1974) pp 59–60.

excuse for inaction. We are not to seek after the experience or to be discouraged if it does not come.

> 'Though God does sometimes withdraw this sense of sweetness, these enthu-
> siastic feelings and these burning desires, he never on that account withdraws
> his grace from his chosen.' (*Epistle of Privy Counsel*, ch 12)

The fact that we pray is sufficient witness to our wanting to pray. The final words should belong to the English mystics:

> 'Lord, you say that no man shall come to you without you, nor shall any man
> be drawn to you unless you draw him. And therefore, Lord, if there be any
> man who is not drawn, I pray you draw him to you. You have drawn me,
> Lord, and I never deserved to be drawn, but according to your great mercy
> you have drawn me.' (*Book of Margery Kempe*, bk 2, ch 10)

> 'When you are about to pray, make your intention and your will at the begin-
> ning as complete and as pure toward God as you can, briefly in you mind, and
> then begin and do as you can. And however badly you are hindered in your
> first resolve, do not be too fearful or angry with yourself, or impatient against
> God for not giving you that savour and spiritual sweetness with devotion
> which (as it seems to you) he gives to other creatures. Instead, see by it your
> own weakness and bear it easily, holding your prayer in your own sight (sim-
> ple as it is) with humbleness of heart, also trusting confidently in the mercy of
> our Lord that he will make it good—more than you know or feel; and if you
> do so, all shall be well.' (*Scale*, bk 1, ch 33)

> 'Do not hang back then, but labour in it until you experience the desire. For
> when you first begin to undertake it, all that you find is a darkness, a sort of
> cloud of unknowing; you cannot tell what it is, except that you experience in
> your will a simple reaching out to God.' (*Cloud*, ch 3)

> 'So I can declare that contemplation is a wonderful enjoying of the love of
> God, and this joy is [a way of] worshipping God which cannot be described.
> And that amazing worship happens within the soul, and because of the over-
> flowing joy and sweetness, it rises up to the mouth, so that the heart and voice
> combine in unison, and the body and soul rejoice in the living God.'
> (*A Form of Living*, ch 12)

9
Bibliography

Walter Hilton	*The Scale of Perfection* (J P H Clark and R Dorwood (ed), Classics of Western Spirituality, New York: Paulist Press, 1991). *The Minor Works of Walter Hilton* (D Jones (ed), London: Burns Oates and Washbourne, 1929).
Margery Kempe	*The Book of Margery Kempe* (B A Windeatt (ed), London: Penguin Classics, 1985)
Julian of Norwich	*Revelations of Divine Love* (C Wolters (ed), London: Penguin Classics, 1966).
Richard Rolle	*The Fire of Love* (C Wolters (ed), London: Penguin Classics, 1972). *The English Writings* (R Allen (ed), Classics of Western Spirituality, London: SPCK, 1989).
Anon	*The Ancrene Riwle* (M B Salu (ed), University of Exeter Press, 1990)
Anon	*The Cloud of Unknowing* (J Walsh (ed), Classics of Western Spirituality, New York: Paulist Press, 1981). *The Cloud of the Unknowing and Other Works* (C Wolters (ed), London: Penguin Classics, 1978).
S Bhattacharji	*God is an Earthquake: the Spirituality of Margery Kempe* (London: Darton, Longman and Todd, 1997)
T Hall	*Too Deep for Words* (New York: Paulist Press, 1991)
D Knowles	*The English Mystical Tradition* (Cardinal Books, London: Burns and Oates, 1961)
T Park	*The English Mystics: An Anthology* (London: SPCK, 1998)
G Pigott	*Prayers to Remember* (Grove Spirituality Series 52, 1995)
M Ramsey	*Canterbury Pilgrim* (London: SPCK, 1974). *Be Still and Know* (London: Fount Paperbacks, 1982).
J Robertson	*Praying with the English Mystics* (London: Triangle, 1990)